LAURENCE KING
First published in Great Britain in 2025 by Laurence King

Text copyright © Laurence King 2025
Illustrations copyright © Alice Pattullo 2025

Alice Pattullo has asserted their right under the Copyright, Designs and Patents Act 1988, to be identified as the illustrator of this work.

All rights reserved. A CIP catalogue record for this book is available from the British Library.

HB ISBN: 978-1-5102-3169-6
E-book ISBN: 978-1-5102-3177-1

10 9 8 7 6 5 4 3 2 1

Printed in China

MIX
Paper | Supporting responsible forestry
FSC® C104740

Laurence King
An imprint of
Hachette Children's Group
Part of Hodder and Stoughton Limited
Carmelite House
50 Victoria Embankment
London EC4Y 0DZ

An Hachette UK Company
www.hachette.co.uk
www.hachettechildrens.co.uk
www.laurenceking.com

The authorised representative in the EEA is Hachette Ireland, 8 Castlecourt Centre, Dublin 15, D15 XTP3, Ireland (email: info@hbgi.ie)

ALL ABOUT MUSHROOMS

Alice Pattullo

⬧ LAURENCE KING

KEEPING YOURSELF AND MUSHROOMS SAFE

Do not ever touch or pick mushrooms you find in the wild. It takes years of study to know which fungi are safe for humans, and many species are poisonous.

When out in the wild, take care not to tread on or kick fungi. If there are fallen branches or dead trees that are not causing any harm or damage, leave them to decompose slowly, as they provide food to fungi. If you are gardening, avoid over-fertilising soil and use native plants.

CONTENTS

What is a Mushroom?	7
How Mushrooms Grow and Spread	8
Where to Find Mushrooms	11
Snowy Disco	12
Mushrooms in Medicine	15
Mushrooms in Food	16
Mushrooms in Folklore	19
Barbie Pagoda	20
Poisonous Fungi	22
Rare Fungi	24
Stinky Fungi	26
Huitlacoche	28
Parts of a Mushroom	31
Colourful Mushrooms	32
Weird Mushrooms	34
Devil's Tooth	36
Partners	38
Large Mushrooms	40
Parasites	42
Juniper-Apple Rust	44
Glossary	46

WHAT IS A MUSHROOM?

Mushrooms are incredible squishy living things that aren't quite plants or animals but aren't quite anything else either. Mushrooms come in all shapes and sizes. The most commonly grown type, the button mushroom, looks like a little white umbrella, and you may have had them for dinner before! Some kinds of mushrooms are familiar foods, and some kinds are poisonous. They are entirely unique – we'd be lost without them!

THE KINGDOM FUNGI

The Latin word for mushroom is *fungus*, but mushrooms are only one type of fungi. Other fungi include moulds, yeasts and lichens.

MORE ANIMAL THAN PLANT

Did you know mushrooms are more like humans then plants? Mushrooms can't produce their own food like plants do, instead growing towards their food sources, similarly to how animals move to find theirs. Like how we communicate online, mushrooms interact with each other using a complex underground network called the Wood Wide Web.

MASTER DECOMPOSERS

Fungi are organisms that live and grow by decomposing and absorbing organic matter. They are nature's rubbish collectors! They break down dead matter and allow it to form new life. We wouldn't exist without mushrooms doing their part in the world's life cycle.

HOW MUSHROOMS GROW AND SPREAD

MAGICAL SPORES

Spores are the structures that mushrooms produce to reach new places. Spores come in all kinds of shapes and sizes. They can be dry or slimy, fuzzy or even jelly-like!

HOW NEW MUSHROOMS ARE MADE

Mushrooms can make new mushrooms by creating spores. Each mushroom has a nucleus cell which holds all the mushroom's genetic material. To make new spores, two nuclei can join together, or one nucleus can split itself multiple times.

HOW MUSHROOMS SPREAD

Mushrooms can release spores into the air in many different incredible ways. Some form the spores inside themselves in sacs called 'asci'. The asci can then disintegrate to make a blob of spores or the mushroom can shoot the spores out of the asci like a water pistol! Once out in the air, the spores can settle nearby or they can be picked up by animals.

GROW, GROW, GROW

Once the spores have landed in the right environment, they can germinate and grow into new mushrooms. Different mushrooms prefer different conditions to grow but most like moisture and staying out of the sun. If the conditions are right, they can grow very quickly, like magic overnight!

GIANT PUFFBALL

PORCINI

COLLARED EARTHSTAR

WHERE TO FIND MUSHROOMS

Mushrooms live in all sorts of places – in the ground, in the air, in the lakes and rivers and seas. Once you start looking, you'll start to see them everywhere.

WHERE DO MUSHROOMS LIVE?

Not all mushrooms are the same – some like to grow in dark shady places, some like to be in light clearings. Some like to grow low down on the ground, others high up in trees. You could even find some growing on your roof! They can be anywhere, but here are some tips for finding them.

> **REMEMBER!**
> **Don't touch** any mushrooms you find, leave them alone so they continue the important work they do!

WHERE TO LOOK

Go to your local wood, park or river and start by looking beneath your feet! Look for any disturbed ground or dead leaves and trees. Mushrooms thrive off decomposing matter, so they will grow close towards it. They also like shady places with a bit of light, so look close to paths and nature trails.

WHEN TO LOOK

The best time to look for mushrooms is autumn. This is when leaves start to fall from the trees and there's lots of dying matter for mushrooms to feast on. They like the cooler temperatures and wetter weather, so go searching after a rainfall.

SNOWY DISCO

FAMILY: LACHNACEAE

DISTRIBUTION: TEMPERATE REGIONS OF EUROPE, ASIA AND NORTH AMERICA

These small white cup fungi are often overlooked; like many of its relatives, it is only when looking at it through a magnifying lens, making its image much larger, that the true beauty of the snowy disco is revealed. These hairy snow-white fungi look as though they have sat through a recent frost. The snowy disco is usually found in groups, on dead and decaying wood, beechnut burs and fir cones.

Lachnum virgineum takes its common name from the no longer used group Discomycetes, which was once used to describe many fungi with a disc-shaped fruiting body. Discomycete spores are kept in a vase-shaped container called an ascus, usually holding eight spores that are forcibly released into the air when they are ready to reproduce.

There are countless other small white, cream or grey cup or disc-like mushrooms that may be confused with one another. A micologist, which is someone who studies mushrooms and fungi, can figure out a species by which season it's growing in, and where in the world it's been found.

KEY CHARACTERISTICS:
- Fruiting bodies are a white disc or flattened cup shape, under 2mm in size.
- The edges of these discs are covered in fine white hairs.
- The discs are attached to their woody substrate by a short stem.

LACHNUM VIRGINEUM

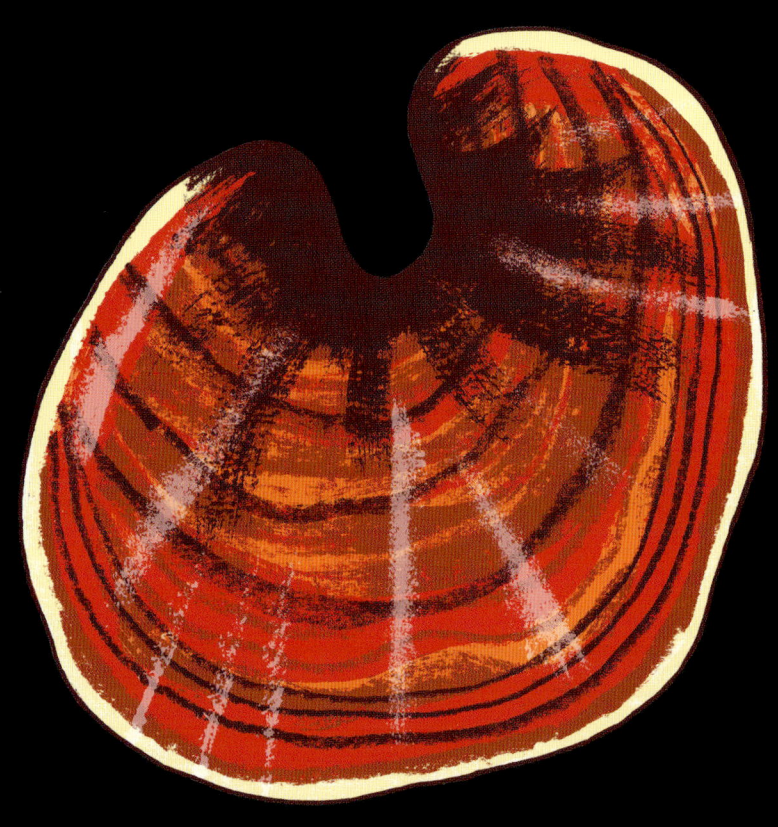

REISHI

MUSHROOMS IN MEDICINE

In 1928 a fungus transformed modern medicine when Alexander Fleming discovered that it could stop bacterial infections. Now scientists are looking for more miracle mushrooms!

ANCIENT MEDICINES

Mushrooms have been used for the healing properties for hundreds of years before Alexander Fleming discovered penicillin in his unwashed petri dishes. The reishi mushroom and the collar earthstar are both used in traditional Chinese medicines while Native American communities grind the fruiting bodies of the scarlet elf cup to dress wounds.

MIRACLE DRUGS

Penicillin changed the modern world when Alexander Fleming discovered it. Since then scientists have looked to fungi for more medicinal properties. One of these is ergot – a type of fungus that causes plant disease. It's used in medicine to help women go into labour when they're having a baby. It also helps to stop bleeding.

FUTURE POSSIBILITIES

Scientists are always looking to mushrooms for potential new medicines. For example, the candlesnuff fungus contains chemical compounds which could be useful in anti-viral medicines or to fight against tumours.

MUSHROOMS IN FOOD

Mushrooms have been delicacies for hundreds of years all over the world! Whether they have a sweeter taste or a more nutty flavour, or they provide a thick texture perfect for bulking out a stew or casserole, mushrooms can often be the key to improving a great meal.

TANTALISING TRUFFLES

Tasty truffles rely on animals wanting to eat them so they can spread and grow. They live underground so they produce a strong, enticing smell to draw animals to them and dig them up. Humans now use dogs and pigs to find delicious truffles for cooking, though truffle hunting with a pig can be risky business – they want to gobble up those tasty truffles themselves! In Italy, pigs haven't been used to hunt for truffles since 1985 as they can damage the mycelia of truffles while digging them up.

MEAT SUBSTITUTES

The beefsteak fungus was named because of its similarity in look and texture to meat. It even oozes red liquid – just like a steak oozes blood! It was once commonly used as meat substitute but isn't as popular nowadays.

COMMON EDIBLE MUSHROOMS

Chanterelle mushrooms were a delicacy favoured by kings and queens in the eighteenth century. Porcini mushrooms are popular among foragers for their flavour while shitake mushrooms count for approximately 25% of all mushroom farming around the world!

PIEDMONT WHITE TRUFFLE

CHANTERELLE

BEEFSTEAK

SHITAKE

MUSHROOMS IN FOLKLORE

The mushroom's tendency to appear almost magically overnight and vanish just as fast has led people to see them as symbols of life and death, omens of good and bad luck or even as bridges to other realms. There is folklore surrounding mushrooms in all parts of the world.

FAIRY CIRCLE

Across Europe, mysterious rings of luscious grass and mushrooms have appeared magically for hundreds of years. In Ireland, these are suspected to be the homes of mischievous fairies. It is considered incredibly bad luck to disturb a fairy circle.

IMMORTALITY

The rare reishi or lingzi mushroom is also known as the 'mushroom of immortality'. In Chinese folklore, emperors and alchemists searched for the mushroom in the hopes of finding eternal youth.

GATEWAYS TO OTHER REALMS

In the depths of forests around the world lives the *Amanita muscaria* – a beautiful red-capped mushroom and perhaps a gateway to another realm . . . Indigenous people in Siberia consumed this mushroom in rituals to communicate with other spiritual worlds. In India, the *Amanita muscaria* is suspected to be the mysterious 'soma' – a sacred drink used to contact the gods.

PROTECTORS

In Slavic folklore, the shapeshifting forest spirit Leshy is believed to appear as a mushroom. Leshy protects the forest but can be mischievous and malevolent. People would ask permission of Leshy before entering his forests. If you anger him, you should try to make him laugh by putting your clothes on backwards!

BARBIE PAGODA

FAMILY: AMYLOCORTICIACEAE

DISTRIBUTION: NEW CALEDONIA, SOUTHWEST PACIFIC OCEAN

The Barbie pagoda was discovered by a local mycological society in New Caledonia in 2009. So far it has not been found anywhere else, meaning it is native to and only grows on the islands.

The common name references its bright pink colour and unique tiers, which resemble a pagoda building. The fruiting body consists of multiple caps, stacked on top of each other and narrowing towards the top, with a fairytale twist of frills. The species name *miranda* comes from the Latin for wonderful – a fitting description.

The tiered shape is unique to the Pagoda fungus genus *Podoserpula*, which only contains two species: the Barbie pagoda and the whitish-cream pagoda fungus. Both grow from the forest floor, which may explain why it looks so different to its relatives the crust fungi, which grow flat against the lower sides of logs and branches. One theory suggests they evolved stems to elevate their caps to catch a breeze to spread their spores. However, the caps lack gills or pores, instead bearing the bumps and folds of their relatives.

KEY CHARACTERISTICS:
- Bright pink in colour.
- A tiered structure reaching up to 10cm high.
- Caps with a texture of irregular bumps and folds.

PODOSERPULA MIRANDA

POISONOUS FUNGI

To keep yourself safe, you should steer clear of anything poisonous. However, not all poisonous mushrooms are deadly. The most dangerous mushrooms have sinister names like Destroying Angel and Funeral Bell.

BLACK MORELS

Black Morels can be edible but are toxic if not cooked correctly – you should only eat them when prepared by an expert.

LIBERTY CAP

The Liberty Cap causes hallucinations, which is when people see things that are not really there, and can be frightening. This common autumn mushroom has been illegal to pick, prepare, eat or sell in the UK since 2005.

DEATH CAP

The Death Cap lives up to its name and is responsible for most mushroom-related deaths due to its similar appearance to many edible mushrooms.

FLY AGARIC

The fairytale-looking Fly Agaric can also cause hallucinations and was traditionally used to kill plant-eating insects.

RARE FUNGI

Some mushrooms are endangered, meaning they are at risk of going extinct and having no living members left. Some species are just very hard to find.

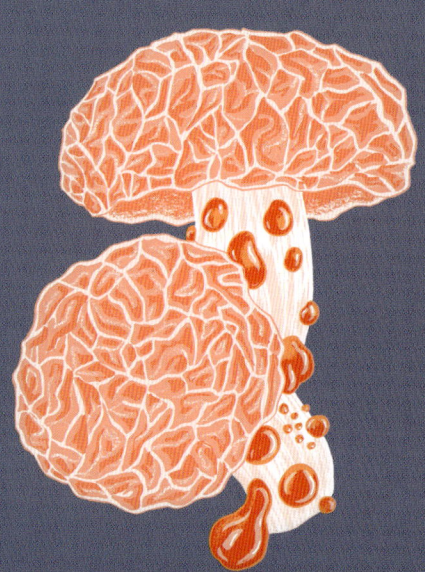

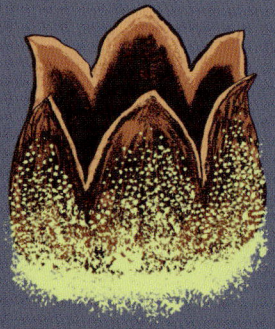

WRINKLED PEACH

The Wrinkled Peach mushroom prefers to grow on elm trees, but as elm tree populations have dwindled due to disease, the Wrinkled Peach mushroom has become extremely rare.

DUNE CUP

Dune Cup fungi grows only on coastal sand dunes, which can be threatened by people walking on them and trampling the vegetation that grows there.

GREEN EARTH TONGUE

Green Earth Tongue mushrooms grow in mossy woodlands and are sensitive to changes within its environment.

BALLERINA WAXCAP

The Ballerina Waxcap grows in fields, lawns and churchyards. As these habitats get made into human developments like housing and car parks, the mushroom's population has declined.

STINKY FUNGI

Some mushrooms produce a smell. Some of these smells are pleasant, like the delicious earthy scent of the Piedmont White Truffle that is a popular food, and the Dryad's Saddle surprisingly smells like a fresh watermelon.

DRYAD'S SADDLE

PIEDMONT WHITE TRUFFLE

Others are less so . . . The Common Stinkhorn has earned its name for the pungent stench it produces, which has been likened to rotting flesh – yuck! Once the fruiting body emerges, the cap oozes a sticky gel containing spores called gleba, which attracts the flies and other insects needed to distribute the spores.

WHITE CAGE FUNGUS

COMMON STINKHORN

HUITLACOCHE

FAMILY: USTILAGINACEAE

DISTRIBUTION: WORLDWIDE

Ustilago maydis is the most well-known species in the smut family, a group of fungi that often cause plant disease. Huitlacoche is also known as corn smut, and as the name suggests, this fungus attacks maize as well as some other grasses. This plant pathogen can kill the corn plant and drastically affect crop yield. Infected plants can be distinguished by the large grey-white galls that form and replace the individual corn kernels, so that the cob looks grotesquely large and strange. The galls eventually split open to reveal dark spores.

Despite its unappetising appearance, corn smut is economically important in Central and South America, where it is considered a delicacy in Mexico's cuisine, traditionally cooked with chopped vegetables. It is thought that this unusual ingredient was utilised by Mesoamerican Aztec people and it continues to be an important food source for indigenous communities. Nutritionally, huitlacoche contains more protein than regular corn kernels, making infected plants highly valuable as a food source. Because corn smut grows quickly in the laboratory, it is also a favourite of scientists looking to study the interactions between fungal plant pathogens and their hosts.

KEY CHARACTERISTICS:
- Parasitises commercially grown maize and some grasses.
- Infected corn kernels grow into galls up to 12 cm in size.
- Galls are usually greenish-white to grey, which erupt to reveal black powdery spores.

USTILAGO MAYDIS

PARTS OF A MUSHROOM

When most people think of a mushroom, they think of spongy cap on top of a stalk, but this is only one tiny part of a much larger organism we can't see.

FRUITING BODY

The fruiting body grows above ground or on a host, like a tree, plant or even an animal. It grows when conditions are right, and the mushroom is ready to reproduce.

MYCELIUM

This is the vast complex web of cells that form underneath the fruiting body like the roots of a plant. It allows the mushroom to seek out food, connect to other mushrooms and make new ones!

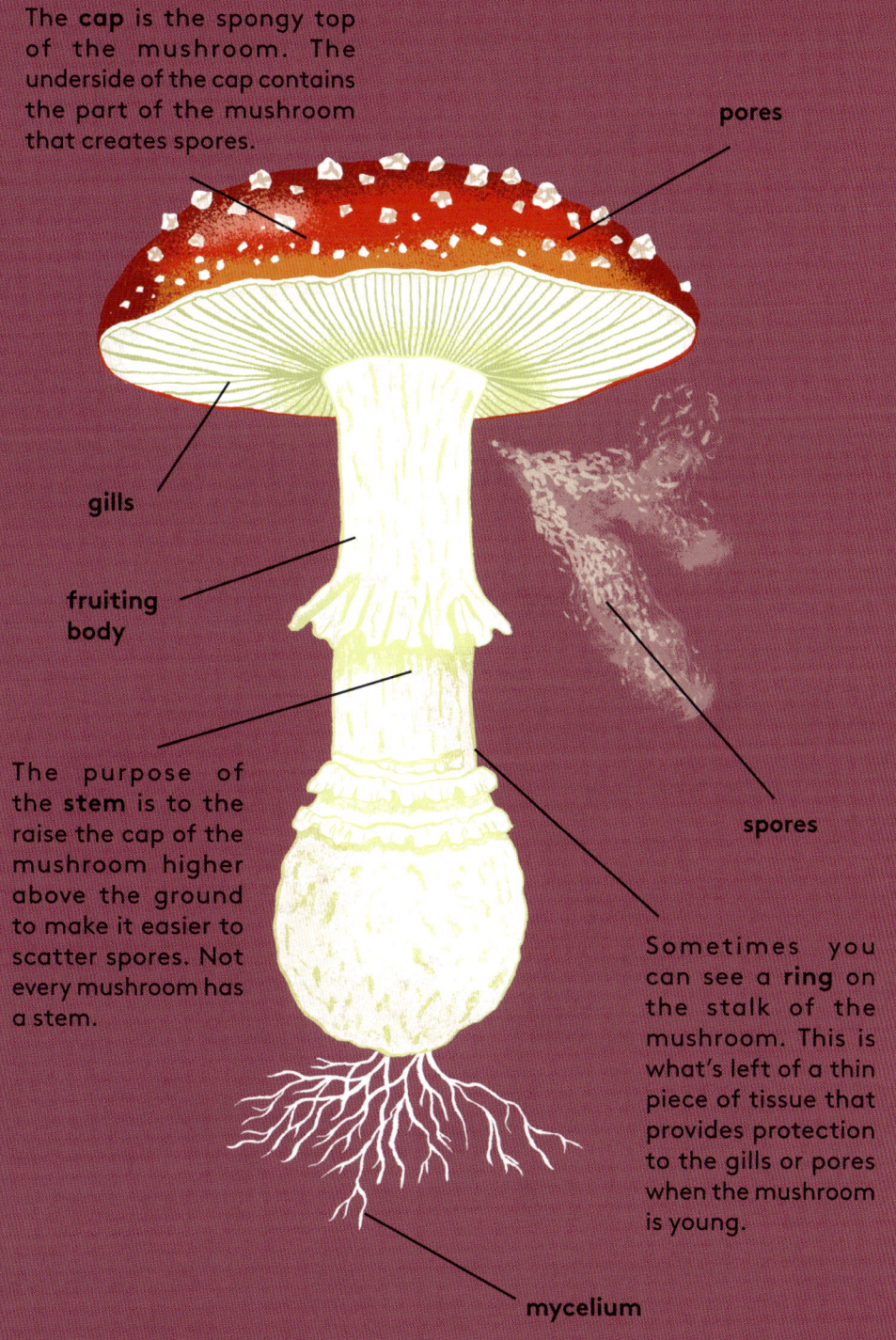

COLOURFUL MUSHROOMS

Mushrooms come in every colour imaginable – even blue, which is one of the rarest colours to find in nature. Mushrooms come so many different colours because they contain pigments. These pigments can serve various purposes, including attracting insects and animals that will help spread spores, warning predators or even just making the environment look more aesthetically pleasing.

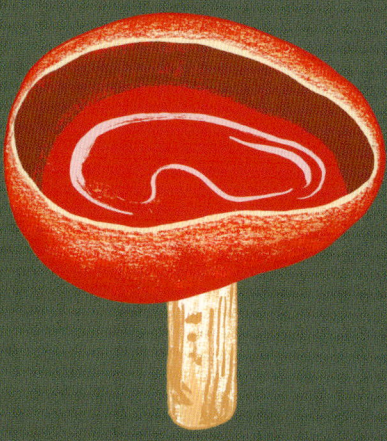

SCARLET ELF CUP

The Scarlet Elf Cup is a bright red/orange colour that looks so similar to another mushroom, the Ruby Elf Cup, that they can only be told apart by looking at both through a microscope.

VERDIGRIS ROUNDHEAD

Verdigris Roundhead is a rare and attractive blue-green mushroom found in Britain and Ireland on lawns, mulch and woodland from spring to autumn.

WERWERE-KŌKAKO

Only the Werewere-Kōkako mushroom and Nessaea aglaura butterfly can produce a true blue pigment!

JADE ELF CUP

Jade Elf cups have striking blue-green cups, usually between 0.5 and 1 cm in size. They start out with high curved edges, which become flatter with age.

WEIRD MUSHROOMS

These mushrooms are so bizarre in appearance that they look like they could have come from another planet!

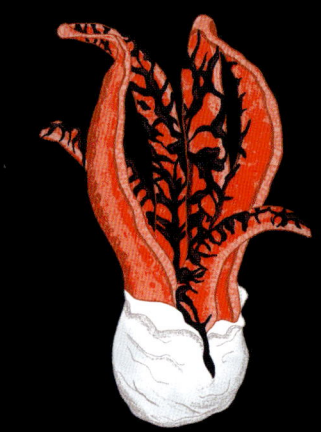

OCTOPUS FUNGUS

The Octopus Fungus in particular looks like an alien with its fruiting body that starts as a cluster of balls and then the tentacles start to push their way out.

COMMON BIRD'S NEST

Common Birds' Nest earned its name by, unsurprisingly, looking like a nest! It can be found growing on decaying wood.

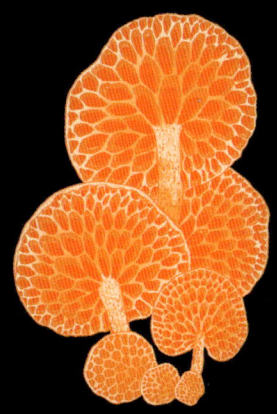

ORANGE PORECAP

The Orange Porecap's cap has an underside that is lighter in colour with oval to hexagonal-shaped large pores that look like honeycomb.

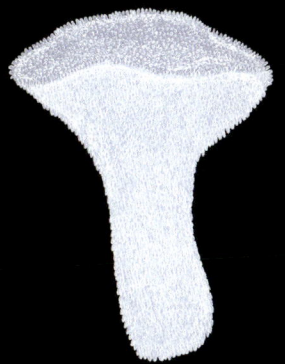

TOOTHED JELLY FUNGUS

Toothed Jelly Fungus looks like a tongue and has teeth-like growths all over the underside.

GREEN PEPE

Green Pepe is slightly translucent, meaning you can partially see through it. It glows at night because it is bioluminescent.

DEVIL'S TOOTH

FAMILY: BANKERACEAE

DISTRIBUTION: NORTH AMERICA, EUROPE

This mushroom is a toothed fungus, which means the material under the cap that releases the spores (the hymenium) resembles small spines or teeth.

Devil's tooth can often be found growing among mosses and pine needle litter in coniferous forests, where they indicate old growth, forming associations with tree hosts once the canopy has closed. Minerals and amino acids are exchanged for carbon from the tree, in a symbiotic relationship.

This strange fungus gets one of its common names, bleeding tooth fungus, from the droplets that form on the surface, which resemble deep red droplets of blood. As the fungus ages it becomes brown and more difficult to identify.

Hydnoid fungi (toothed fungi) have been in decline since the 1950s, right across Europe. This is likely due to increasing pollution causing excess nitrogen in the soil, rendering the fungus' purpose obsolete as the tree no longer requires it for nutrients. This fungus is also prized by mushroom dyers, who use it to create various colours.

KEY CHARACTERISTICS:
- Spore-producing structure is made up of 'teeth' or spines.
- Displays guttation (bleeds red juice).
- Found among mosses and leaf litter in coniferous forests.

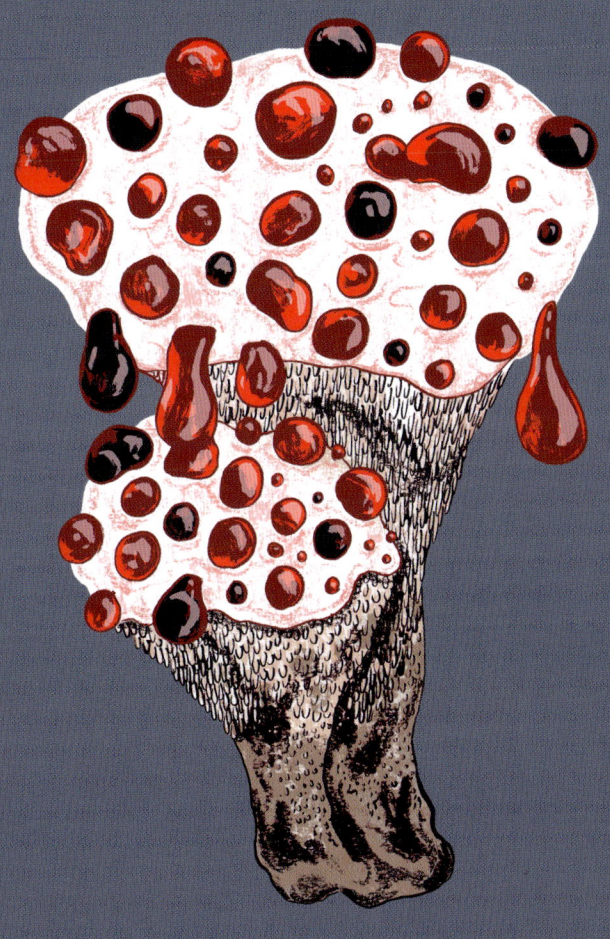

HYDNELLUM PECKII

PARTNERS

These mushrooms form a 'symbiotic' relationship with the roots of plants and trees. That means that both the mushroom and the plant get something good out of joining together, whether that is food or increased chances of survival.

INDIGO MILK CAP

The Indigo Milk Cap is named for its blue fruiting body and the milky blue latex that oozes out of it when it is cut open.

REINDEER CUP LICHEN

A lichen is a symbiotic relationship between a fungi and a photosynthetic partner like an algae. The fungus provides structure for the photosynthetic partner, which in turn provides food.

AMETHYTST DECIEVER

The Amethyst Deceiver is a beautiful purple colour when younger, but its brightness fades as it gets older, making it more difficult to identify with age – this is where the 'deceiver' name comes from.

BARE-TOOTHED RUSSUIA

Bare-toothed Russulas are ectomycorrhizal, meaining they form partnerships with trees. The Russula improves soil resource uptake for the tree while the tree provides carbon dioxide.

LARGE MUSHROOMS

Mushrooms come in all shapes and size but these ones can grow very large!

LION'S MANE

The Lion's Mane fungus usually grows on hardwoods, mostly feeding on dead maple and beech trees. They produce long spines that resemble a beard.

GIANT PUFFBALL

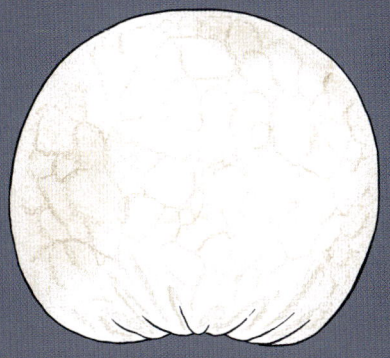

The Giant Puffball grows on forest floors and can easily be mistake for a lost football! Its pure white inside and can be very tasty if eaten when it's young.

SALMON GUM

The Salmon Gum is the largest mushroom found in Australia, and one of the biggest in the world. The biggest ever found weighed 29 kilograms – that's about the weight of a 9-year-old child!

PARASITES

Some mushrooms are parasites, which means that they feed off a living host to survive.

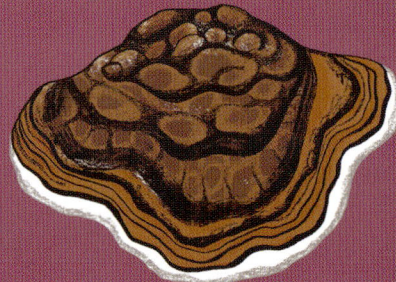

JELLY EAR

Jelly Ear often grows on old and dead wood. It has a jelly-like texture when young and has tiny hairs covering the top of the fungus.

ARTIST'S BRACKET

Artist's Bracket are tough, hard and woody. Scratching the creamy white underside leaves a brown mark, which allows someone to produce writing and drawings.

TARANTULA CORDYCEPS

Cordyceps invade and eat the bodies of arthropods such as insects, spiders and their relatives, with the Tarantula Cordyceps feeding off, you guessed it, tarantulas.

ZOMBIE ANT FUNGUS

The Zombie Ant Fungus infects an ant and then makes it climb up a leaf and bite it so that it's in the best position to release spores.

JUNIPER-APPLE RUST

FAMILY: GYMNOSPORANGIACEAE

DISTRIBUTION: NORTH AMERICA

Juniper-apple rust is a member of a large group of fungi that cause plant diseases, named for the easily visible brown–orange 'rusty' coloured powdery spores they produce on plant surfaces.

Rusts are needed to infect a living plant to complete their life cycle. Like many other rust fungi, the Juniper-apple rust requires more than one host plant and will cycle between two different hosts; junipers and, preferentially, apple trees. When this rust develops on a species of *Juniperus* it appears as brown galls, which swell over time then erupt after rain, producing masses of bright-orange jelly textured horns. These horns release spores, then dry, shrivel up and drop off.

The released spores must then infect a secondary host, a species in the rose family, to complete its life cycle (usually apples, pears or quince). Once infected, yellow spots appear on the apple leaves, with the undersides of the leaves covered in the darker spore producing part of the fungus. Young fruit can also become infected, exhibiting a circular formation of orange-yellow spots, often affecting crop yield, making the juniper-apple rust an economically important plant pathogen.

KEY CHARACTERISTICS:
- On *Juniperus* large galls form, producing gelatinous, orange, tentacle-like horns when mature.
- On apples and other hosts, yellow or dark spots appear, often in a circular pattern, on leaves and young fruit.

GYMNOSPORANGIUM
JUNIPERI-VIRGINIANAE

GLOSSARY

Algae – organisms that live mainly in water and make their food from sunlight by photosynthesis. Algae are very important because they make much of Earth's oxygen.

Bacteria – small organisms that can be found of all natural environments, that are made of a single cell. Some bacteria are good for us, while some are bad.

Bacterial infection – the presence of harmful bacteria in a living species.

Cell – the smallest unit with the basic properties of life. Human beings are made up of more than 75 trillion cells.

Coniferous – woody evergreens that have cones and needles rather than leaves, e.g. a pine or fir tree.

Decay – the process of slowly losing quality, strength or health.

Decomposing – breaking down into smaller parts, e.g. when a substance starts to break down and decay.

Disintegrate – to come apart; break down into pieces or parts.

Evergreen – plants that never lose their leaves, cones or needles and 'stay green' all year long.

Family – a group of living things that share a common feature or characteristic.

Fungus – a simple living organism that is neither a plant or animal. When there is more than one fungus they are called fungi.

Germinate – when a seed breaks open and a plant emerges.

Lichens – made up of two living things: a fungus and an alga (algae).

Mould – a form of fungus, larger than yeast but lacking the large, visible structures that mushrooms have.

Nucleus – the main control centre for the cell, acting like the cell's brain.

Organic matter – matter that has come from a recently living organism.

Organisms – any living thing, e.g. plants, animals and fungi.

Pagoda – a tower in eastern Asia with multiple storeys and eaves.

Parasite – an organism that lives on or inside another organism to get food and other things it needs. The basic relationship is always the same – good for the parasite, harmful for the host.

Pathogen – tiny living things that cause infectious diseases. They can also be called germs.

Photosynthesis – the process in which plants take the energy from sunlight to make their own food.

Symbiosis – when one organism has a close relationship with another organism.

Yeasts – tiny one-celled organisms. Some are harmful to humans, but most are useful, especially in making bread and other food and drinks.